FAVORITE ANIMALS IN
ORIGAMI

John Montroll

DOVER PUBLICATIONS, INC.
Mineola, New York

Bibliographical Note

Favorite Animals in Origami is a new work, first published by Dover Publications, Inc., in 1996.

Library of Congress Cataloging-in-Publication Data

Montroll, John.
    Favorite animals in origami / John Montroll.
        p. cm.
    ISBN-13: 978-0-486-29136-9 (pbk.)
    ISBN-10: 0-486-29136-7 (pbk.)
        1. Origami. 2. Animals in art. I. Title.
TT870.M555 1996
736'.982—dc20
                                                96-14937
                                                CIP

Manufactured in the United States by Courier Corporation
29136714
www.doverpublications.com

Introduction

Of all the possible models to fold, mammals are among my favorites. Here is a collection of a dozen mammals ranging in skill level from intermediate to high-intermediate.

The diagrams follow the internationally approved Randlett–Yoshizawa style, which is easy to follow once you have learned the basic folds. You can use any kind of square paper for these models, but the best results and most precise folding can be achieved using standard origami paper, which is colored on one side and white on the other. In these diagrams, the shading represents the colored side. Origami paper can be found in many hobby shops or purchased by mail from Origami USA, a non-profit organization of dedicated paperfolders. For more information about the group, send a self-addressed, business-size envelope with two first-class stamps to:

> Origami USA
> 15 West 77th St.
> New York, NY 10024–5192

Origami paper, and a catalog of other available craft books, can also be ordered from Dover Publications, Inc., at:

> Dover Publications, Inc.
> 31 East 2nd St.
> Mineola, NY 11501

I hope you enjoy folding these as much as I did creating them.

John Montroll

Contents

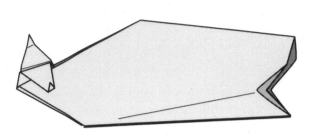

Whale
Page 9

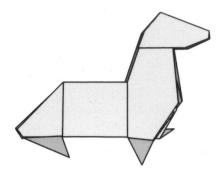

Seal
Page 11

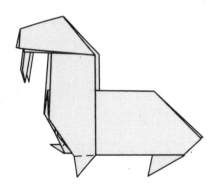

Walrus
Page 14

Squirrel
Page 17

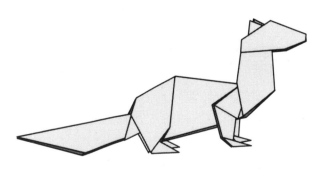

Mink
Page 20

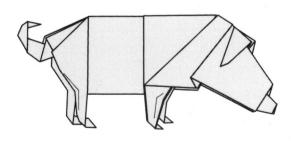

Pig
Page 24

Llama
Page 27

Deer
Page 30

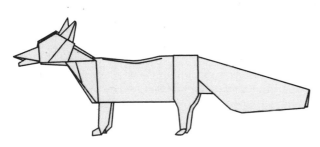

Fox
Page 34

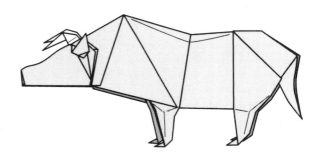

Bull
Page 38

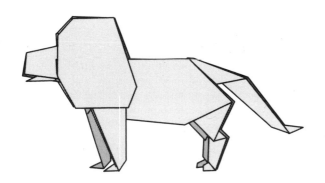

Lion
Page 42

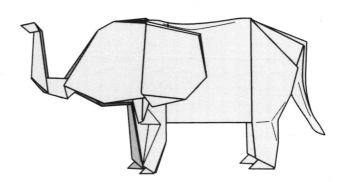

Elephant
Page 45

Contents 5

Symbols

Lines

— — — — — — — — —   Valley fold, fold in front.

—·—·—·—·—·—   Mountain fold, fold behind.

———————————   Crease line.

························   X-ray or guide line.

Arrows

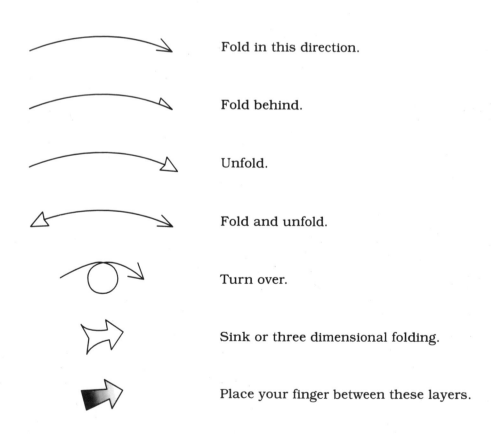

Fold in this direction.

Fold behind.

Unfold.

Fold and unfold.

Turn over.

Sink or three dimensional folding.

Place your finger between these layers.

Basic Folds

Rabbit Ear.

To fold a rabbit ear, one corner is folded in half and laid down to a side.

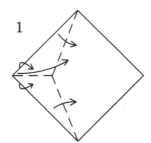

1

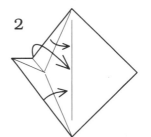

2

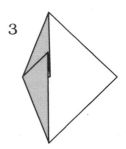

3

Fold a rabbit ear.

A three-dimensional intermediate step.

Double Rabbit Ear.

If you were to bend a straw you would be folding the double rabbit ear.

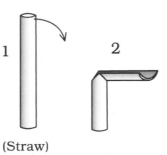

1

2

(Straw)

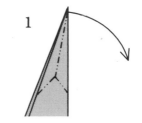

1

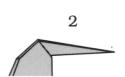

2

Make a double rabbit ear.

Squash Fold.

In a squash fold, some paper is opened and then made flat. The shaded arrow shows where to place your finger.

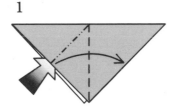

1

Squash-fold.

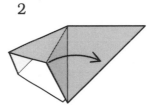

2

A three-dimensional intermediate step.

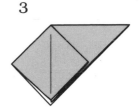

3

Petal Fold.

In a petal fold, one point is folded up while two opposite sides meet each other.

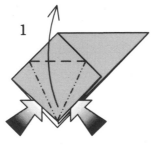

1

Petal-fold.

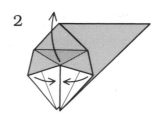

2

A three-dimensional intermediate step.

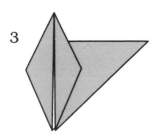

3

Inside Reverse Fold.

In an inside reverse fold, some paper is folded between layers. Here are two examples.

Reverse-fold.

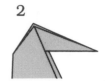

Reverse-fold.

Outside Reverse Fold.

Much of the paper must be unfolded to make an outside reverse fold.

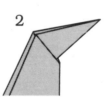

Outside-reverse-fold.

Crimp Fold.

A crimp fold is a combination of two reverse folds.

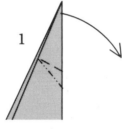

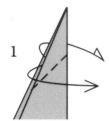

Crimp-fold.

Sink Fold.

In a sink fold, some of the paper without edges is folded inside. To do this fold, much of the model must be unfolded.

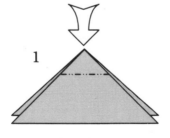

Sink.

Spread Squash Fold.

A cross between a squash fold and a sink fold; some paper in the center is spread apart and then made flat.

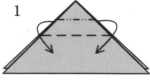

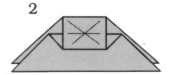

Spread-squash-fold.

Whale

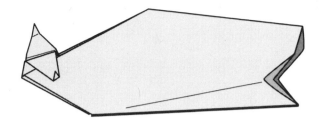

1

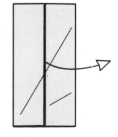

Fold and unfold.

2

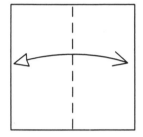

3

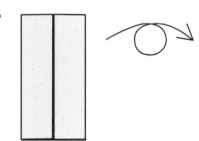

4

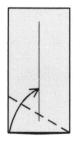

Fold the corner to
the center line.

5

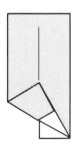

6

7

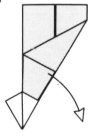

Unfold.

8

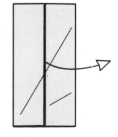

Unfold.

9

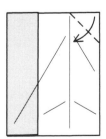

10

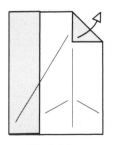

Unfold.

11

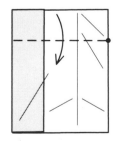

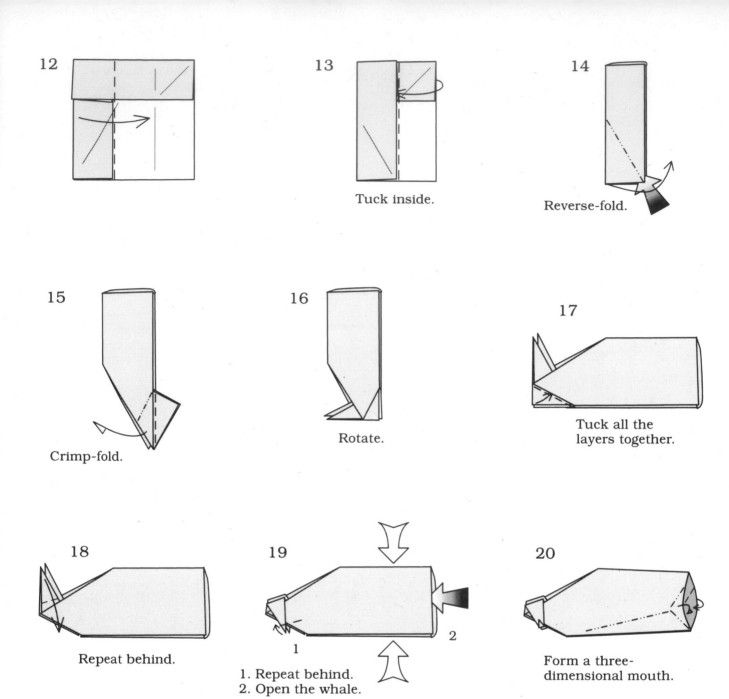

12

13

Tuck inside.

14

Reverse-fold.

15

Crimp-fold.

16

Rotate.

17

Tuck all the
layers together.

18

Repeat behind.

19

1. Repeat behind.
2. Open the whale.

20

Form a three-
dimensional mouth.

21

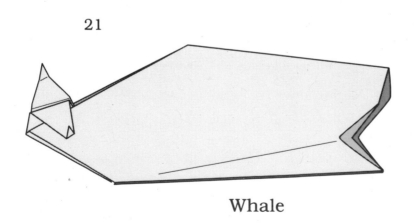

Whale

Seal

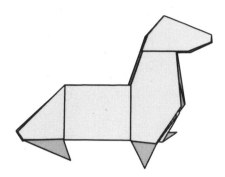

1

Fold and unfold
along the diagonal.

2

Kite-fold.

3

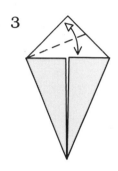

Fold and unfold.

4

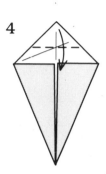

5

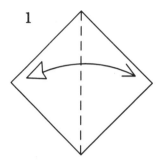

6

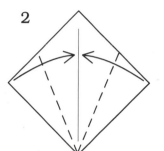

7

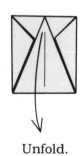

Unfold.

8

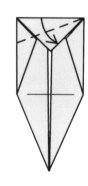

9

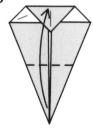

Unfold.

10

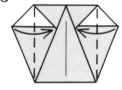

11

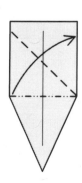

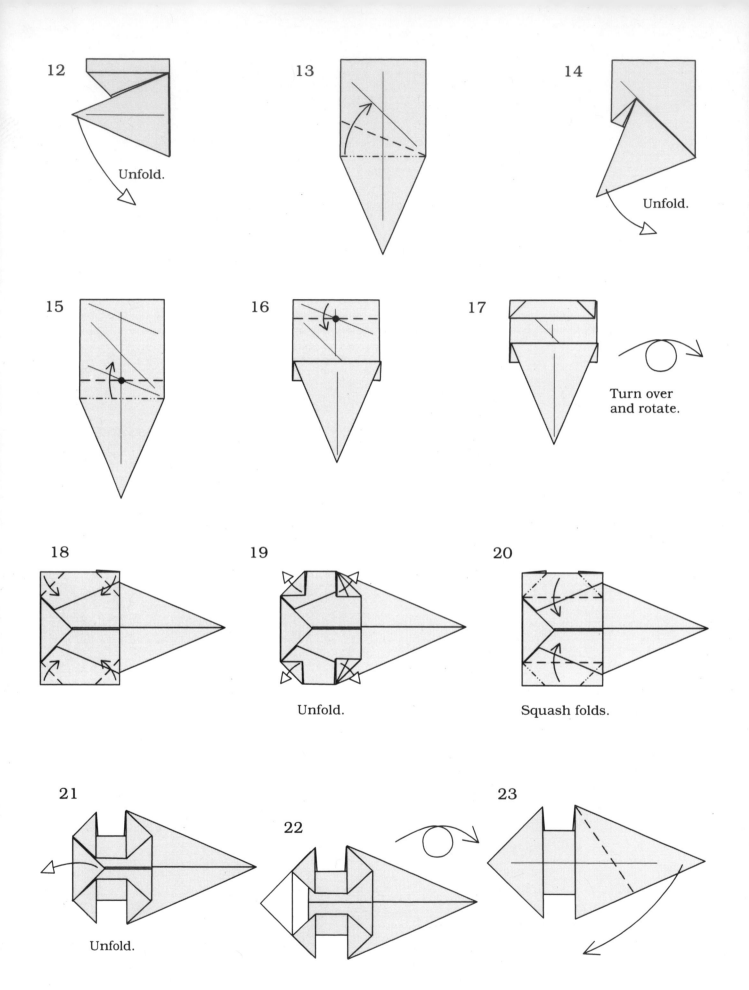

12   Unfold.

13

14   Unfold.

15

16

17   Turn over and rotate.

18

19   Unfold.

20   Squash folds.

21   Unfold.

22

23

24

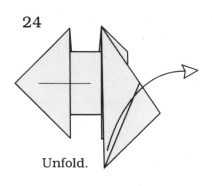

Unfold.

25

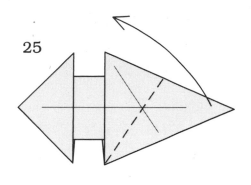

26

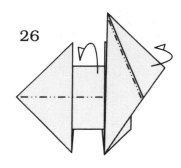

27

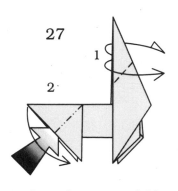

1. Outside-reverse-fold.
2. Reverse-fold.

28

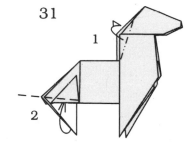

Sink.

29

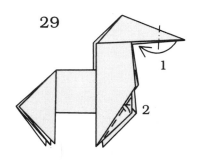

1. Reverse-fold.
2. Tuck inside, repeat behind.

30

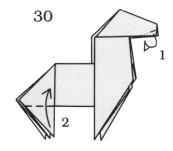

Repeat behind.

31

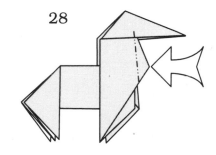

1. Repeat behind.
2. Tuck inside.

32

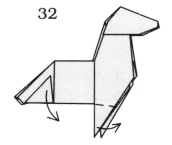

Fold the legs out,
repeat behind.

33

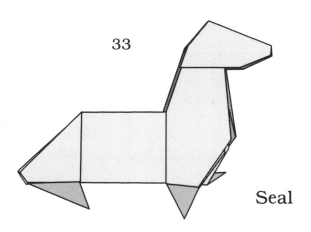

Seal

Walrus

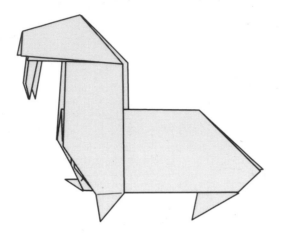

1

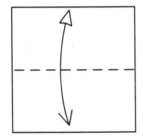

Fold and unfold.

2

3

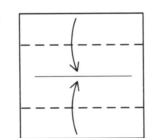

4

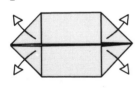

Unfold.

5

6

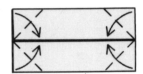

7

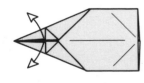

Unfold.

8

Reverse-fold.

9

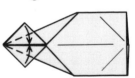

Reverse-fold.

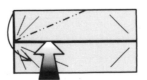

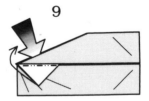

10

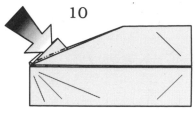

Reverse-fold.

11

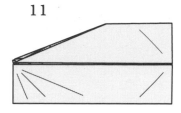

Repeat steps
8–10 below.

12

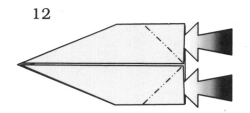

Reverse folds.

13

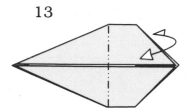

Fold and unfold.

14

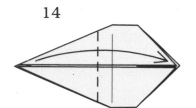

15

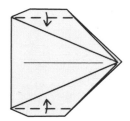

16

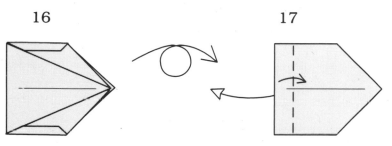

17

Fold on the crease.

18

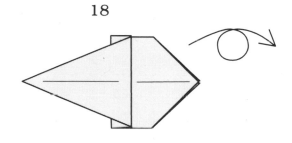

19

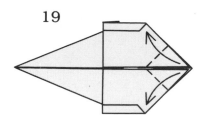

20

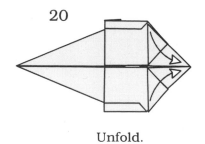

Unfold.

21

Squash folds.

22

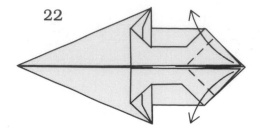

23

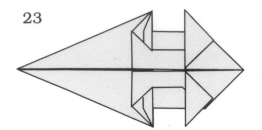

24

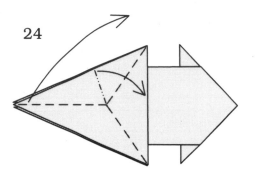

Rabbit-ear.

25

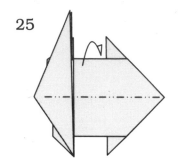

26 1

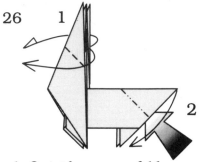

2

1. Outside-reverse-fold.
2. Reverse-fold.

27

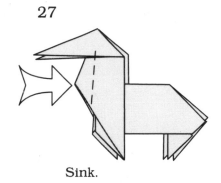

Sink.

28

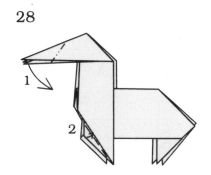

1. Reverse-fold.
2. Tuck inside.
Repeat behind.

29

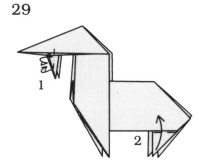

Repeat behind.

30

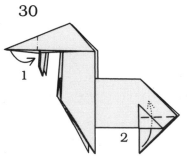

1. Reverse-fold.
2. Tuck inside.

31

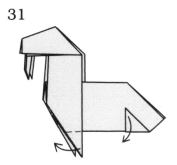

Fold the legs out,
repeat behind.

32

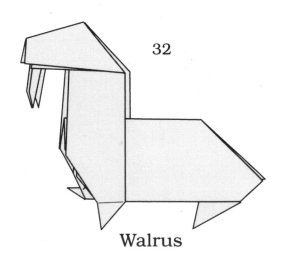

Walrus

Squirrel

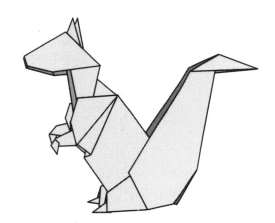

1

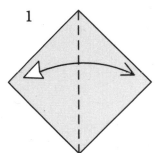

Fold and unfold
along the diagonal.

2

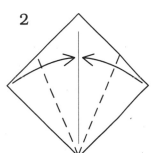

3

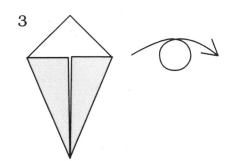

4

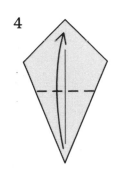

5

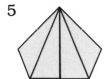

6

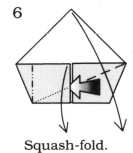

Squash-fold.

7

Squash-fold.

8

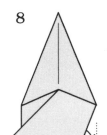

Pull out.

9

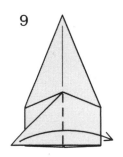

10

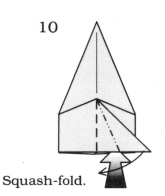

Squash-fold.

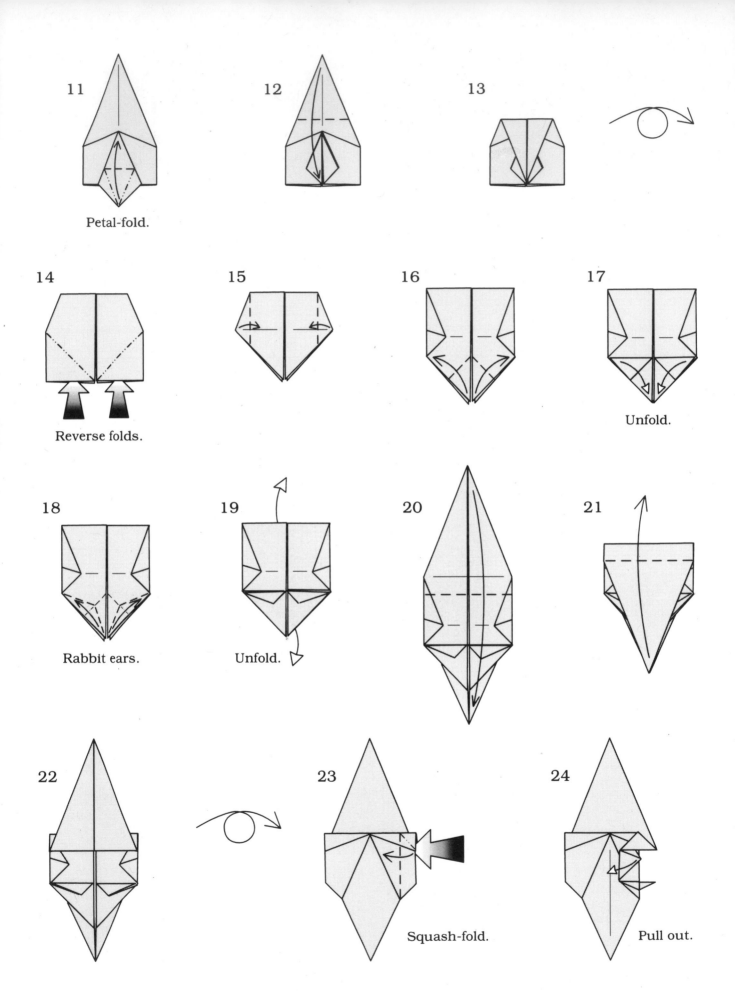

11

Petal-fold.

12

13

14

Reverse folds.

15

16

17

Unfold.

18

Rabbit ears.

19

Unfold.

20

21

22

23

Squash-fold.

24

Pull out.

25

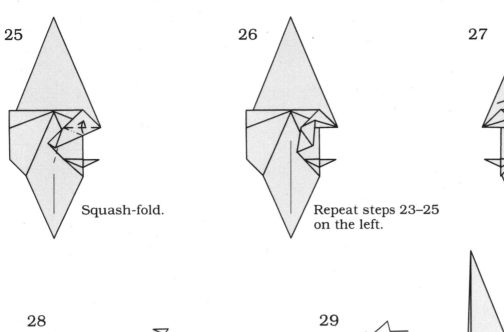

Squash-fold.

26

Repeat steps 23–25
on the left.

27

Fold in half
and rotate.

28

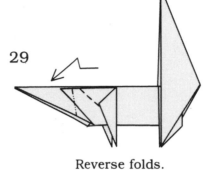

Outside-reverse-fold.

29

Reverse folds.

30

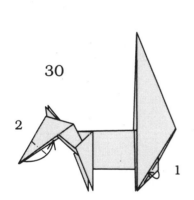

2

1

1. Tuck inside, repeat behind.
2. Reverse-fold.

31

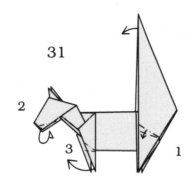

2

3

1

1. Crimp-fold.
2. Mountain-fold.
3. Crimp-fold.
Repeat behind.

32

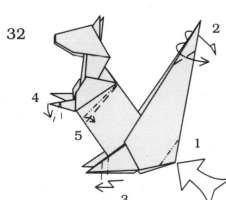

2

4

5

1

3

1. Sink.
2. Outside-reverse-fold.
3. Crimp-fold.
4. Squash-fold.
5. Crimp-fold.
Repeat behind.

33

Squirrel

Mink

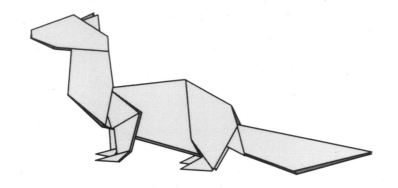

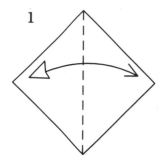

1

Fold and unfold
along the diagonal.

2

3

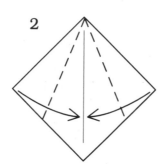

Unfold.

4

5

6

7

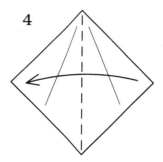

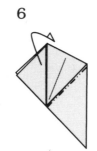

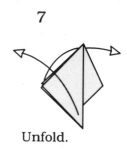

Unfold.

8

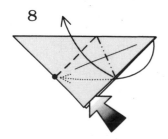

Squash-fold.

9

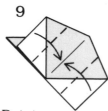

Rotate.

10

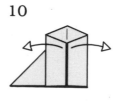

Unfold.

11

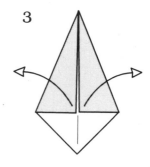

Petal-fold.

12

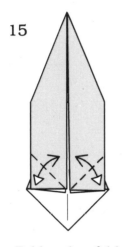

13

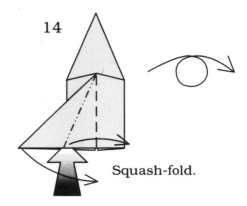

14

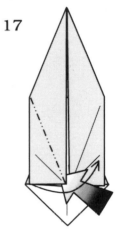

Squash-fold.

15

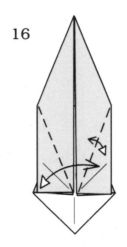

Fold and unfold.

16

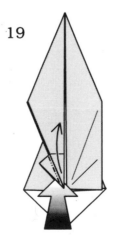

Fold and unfold.

17

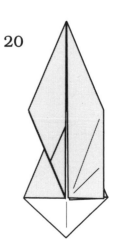

Reverse-fold.

18

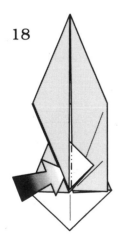

Reverse-fold.

19

Squash-fold.

20

Repeat steps 17–19
on the right.

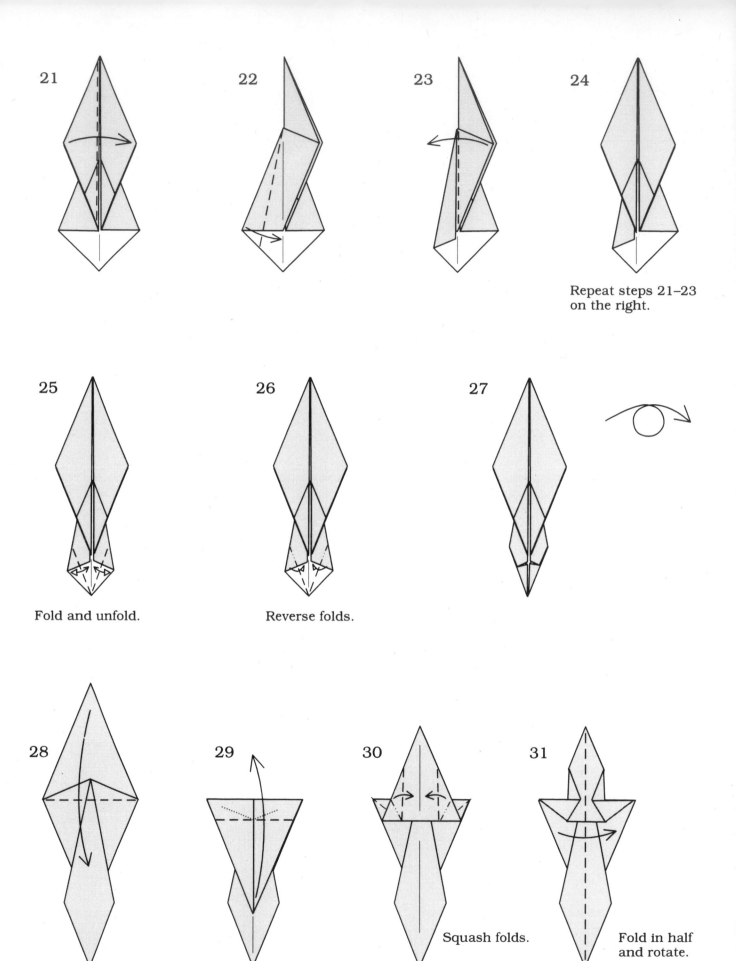

21

22

23

24

Repeat steps 21–23
on the right.

25

Fold and unfold.

26

Reverse folds.

27

28

29

30

Squash folds.

31

Fold in half
and rotate.

32

Reverse-fold,
repeat behind.

33

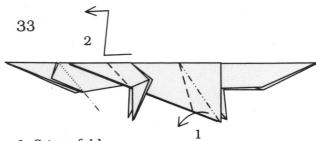

1. Crimp-fold.
2. Outside reverse-folds.

34

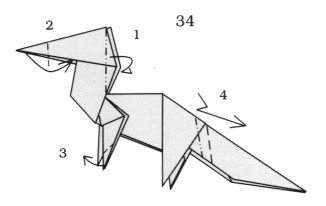

1. Repeat behind.
2. Reverse-fold.
3. Outside-reverse-fold,
   repeat behind.
4. Crimp-fold.

35

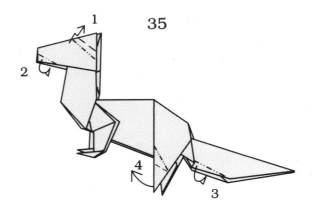

4. Crimp-fold.
Repeat behind.

36

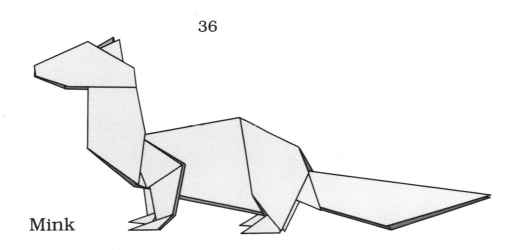

Mink

Pig

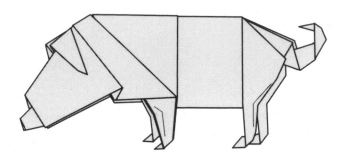

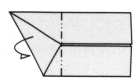

1

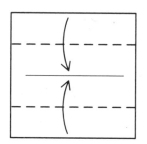

2

3

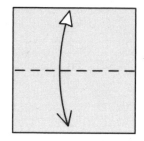

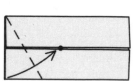

4

5

Fold and unfold.

6

Fold to the crease
while unfolding the
paper from behind.

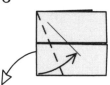

7

Unfold.

8

9

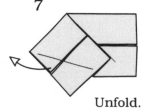

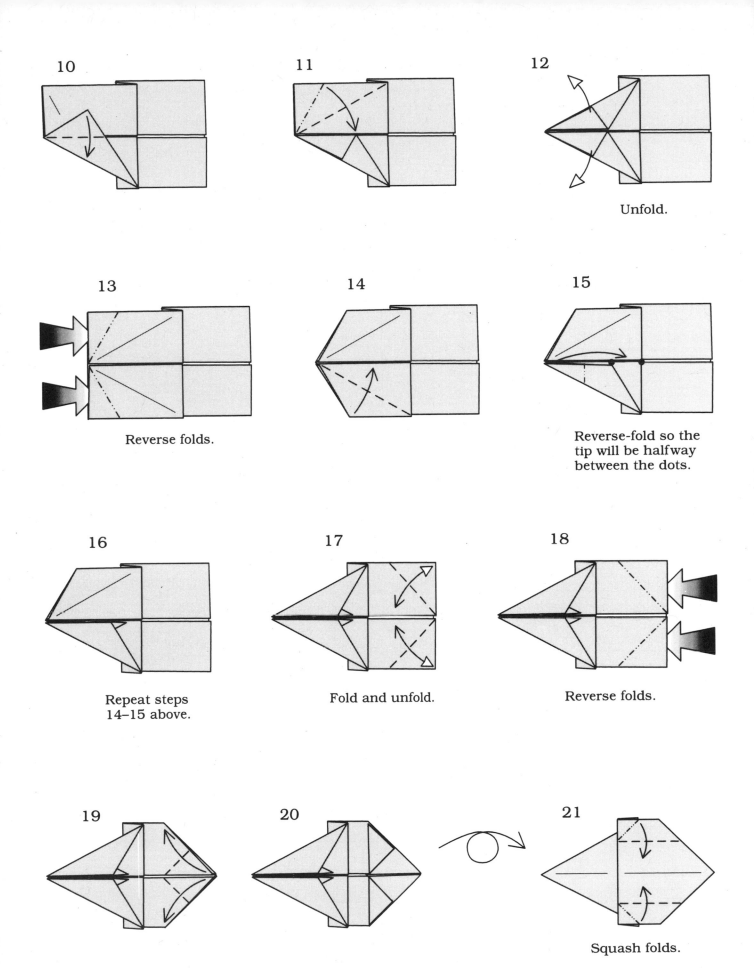

10

11

12

Unfold.

13

Reverse folds.

14

15

Reverse-fold so the
tip will be halfway
between the dots.

16

Repeat steps
14–15 above.

17

Fold and unfold.

18

Reverse folds.

19

20

21

Squash folds.

22

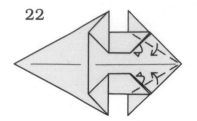

23

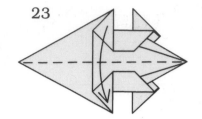

24

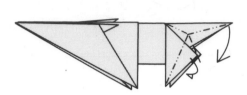

Double-rabbit-ear.

25

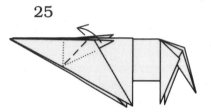

Repeat behind.

26

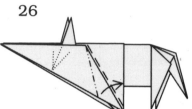

Crimp-fold.

27

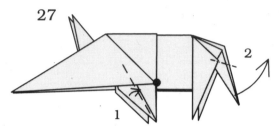

1. Tuck inside, repeat behind.
2. Reverse-fold.

28

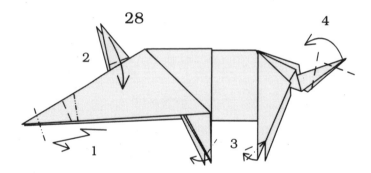

Repeat behind.

29

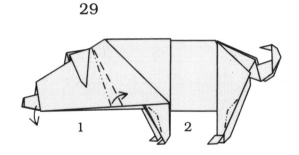

1. Crimp-fold.
2. Shape the legs,
   repeat behind.

30

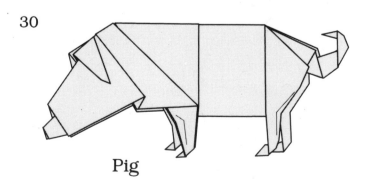

Pig

Llama

1

Fold and unfold.

2

3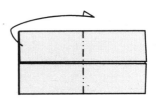

4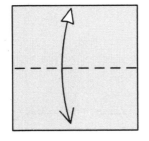

5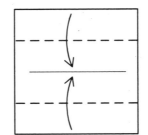

Unfold.

6

7

8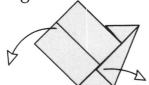

Unfold.

9

10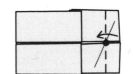

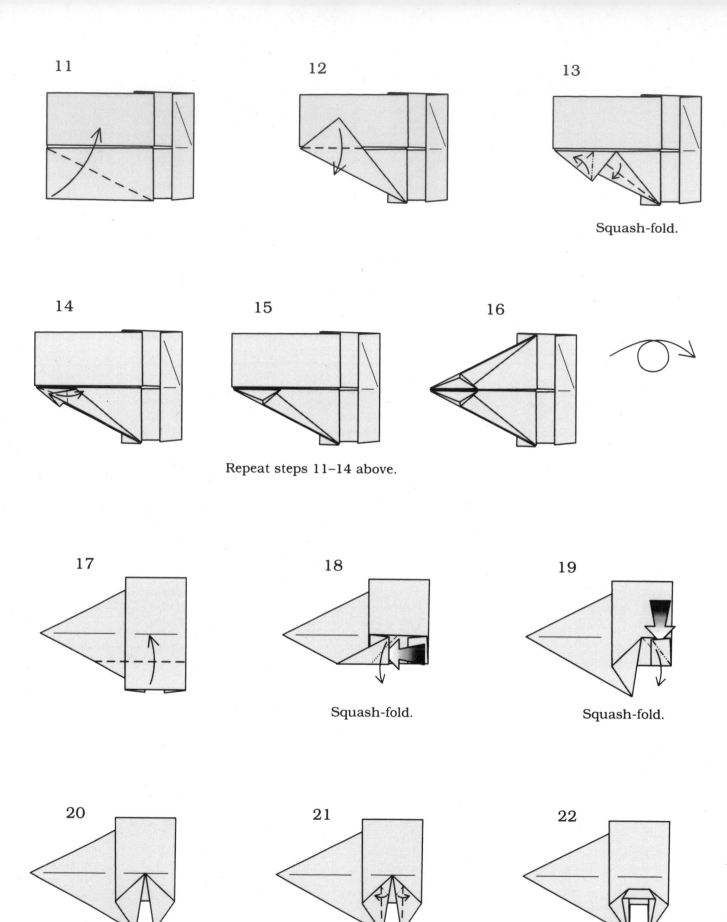

11

12

13

Squash-fold.

14

15

16

Repeat steps 11–14 above.

17

18

Squash-fold.

19

Squash-fold.

20

21

22

Repeat steps 17–21 above.

23

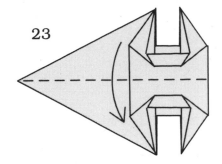

24

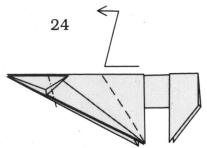

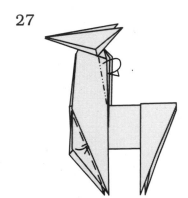

Outside-reverse folds.

25

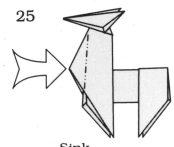

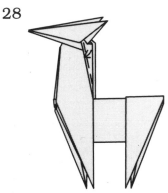

Sink.

26

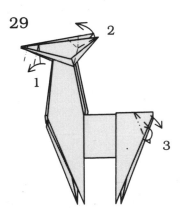

Repeat behind.

27

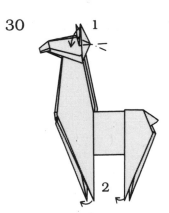

Tuck inside,
repeat behind.

28

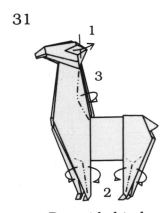

Repeat behind.

29

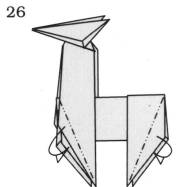

1. Crimp-fold.
2. Rabbit-ear, repeat behind.
3. Crimp-fold.

30

1. Squash-fold.
2. Make little hooves.
Repeat behind.

31

Repeat behind.

32

Llama

Deer

1

Fold and unfold.

2

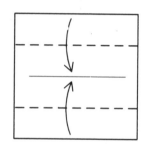

3

4

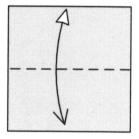

5

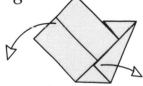

Unfold.

6

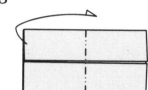

7

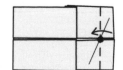

8

Unfold.

9

10

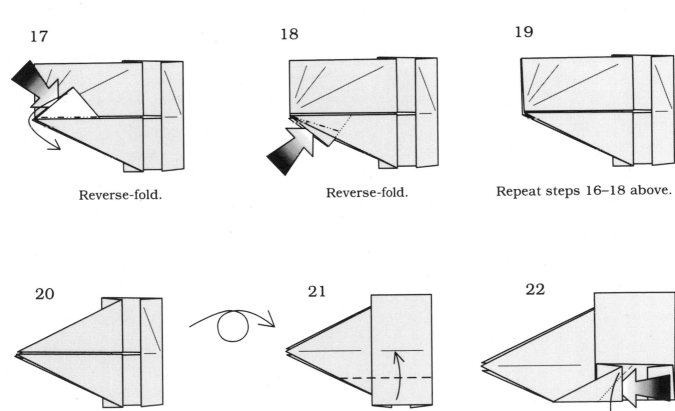

11

12

13

14

15

Unfold.

16

Reverse-fold.

17

Reverse-fold.

18

Reverse-fold.

19

Repeat steps 16–18 above.

20

21

22

Squash-fold.

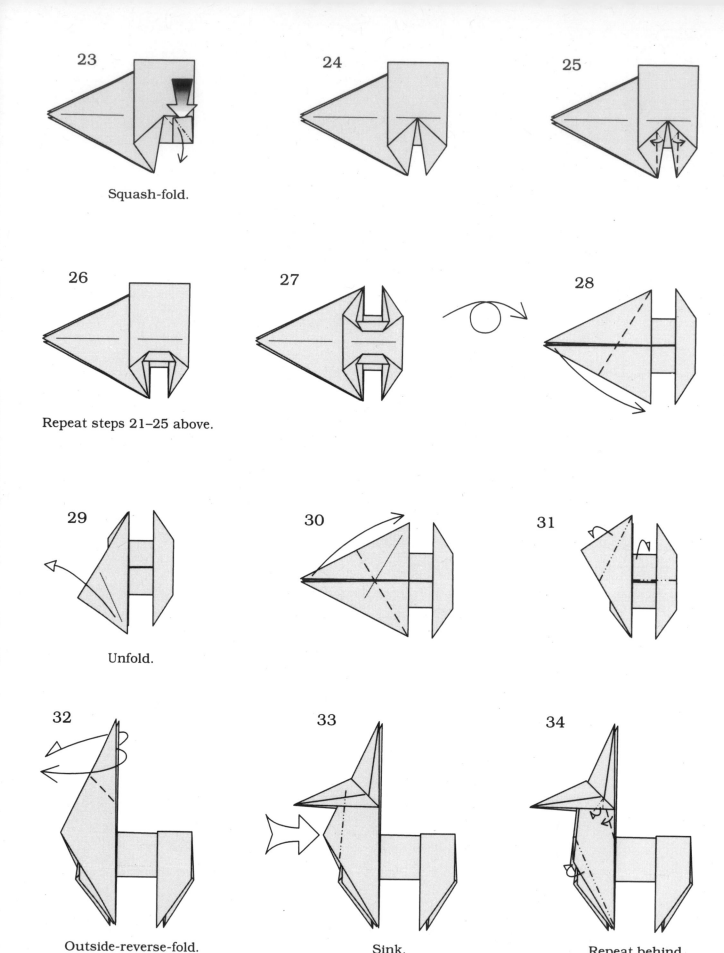

23 Squash-fold.

24

25

26 Repeat steps 21–25 above.

27

28

29 Unfold.

30

31

32 Outside-reverse-fold.

33 Sink.

34 Repeat behind.

35

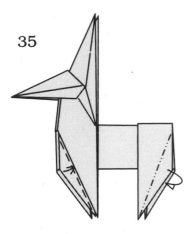

Repeat behind.

36

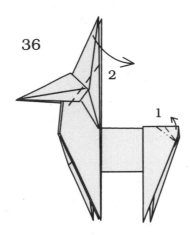

1. Crimp-fold.
2. Repeat behind.

37

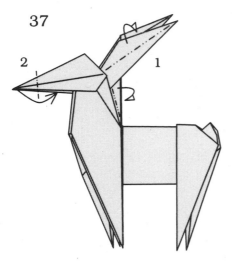

1. Repeat behind.
2. Reverse-fold.

38

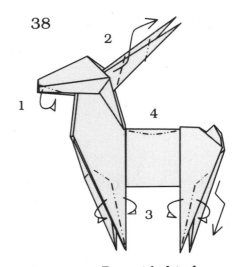

Repeat behind.

39

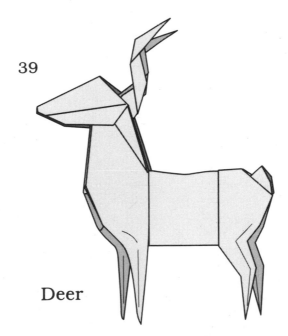

Deer

Fox

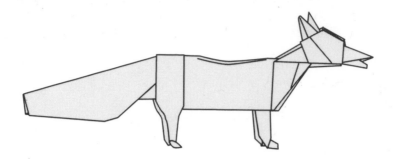

1

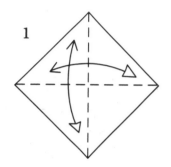

Fold and unfold
along the diagonals.

2

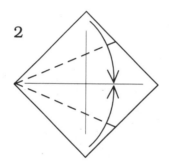

3

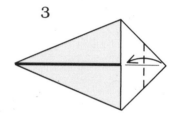

4

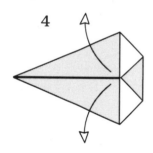

Unfold.

5

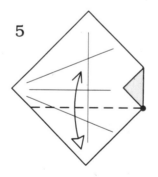

Fold up and unfold.

6

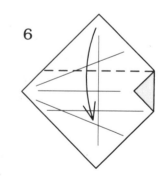

7

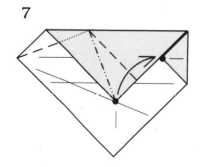

Squash-fold.

8

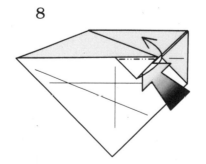

Reverse-fold.

9

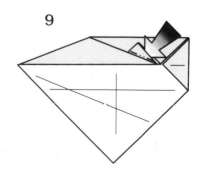

Reverse-fold.

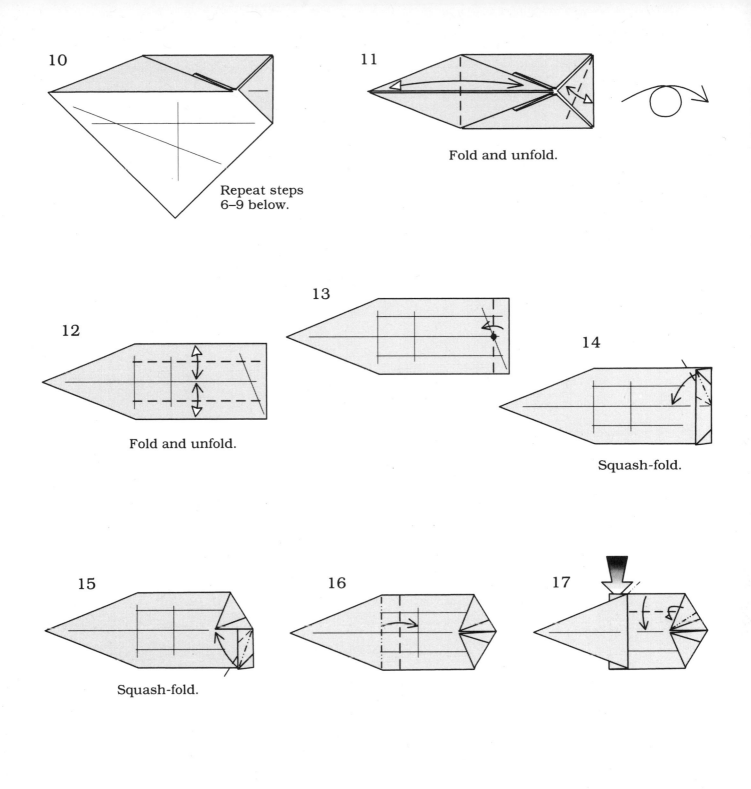

10

Repeat steps
6–9 below.

11

Fold and unfold.

12

Fold and unfold.

13

14

Squash-fold.

15

Squash-fold.

16

17

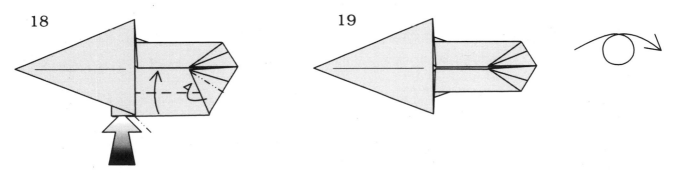

18

19

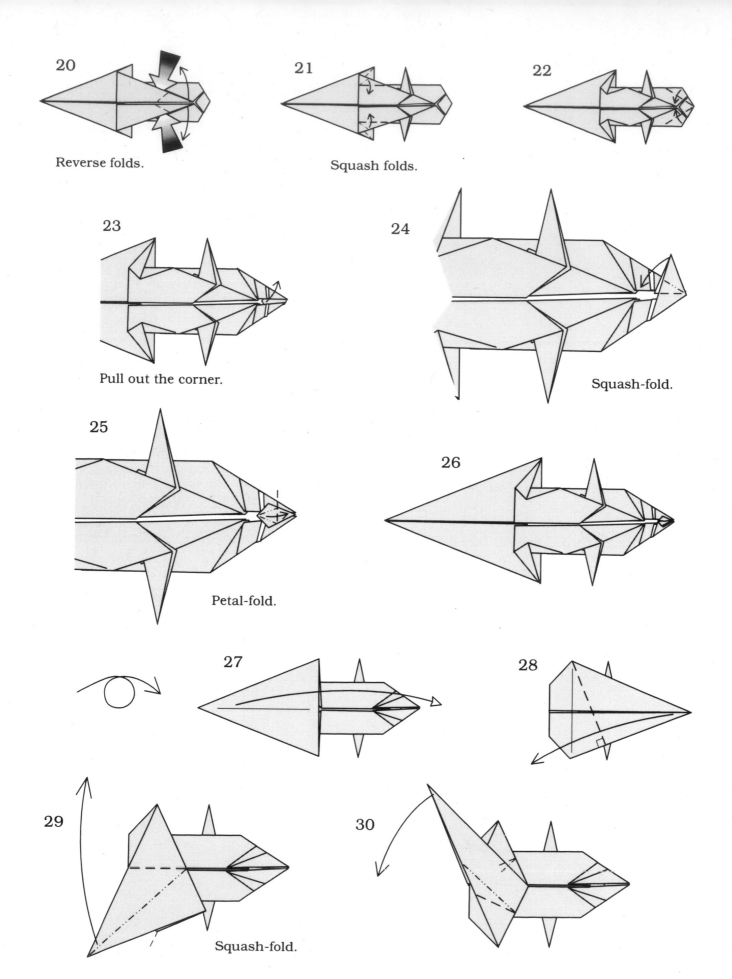

20

Reverse folds.

21

Squash folds.

22

23

Pull out the corner.

24

Squash-fold.

25

Petal-fold.

26

27

28

29

Squash-fold.

30

31

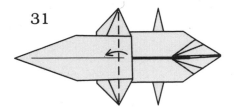

32

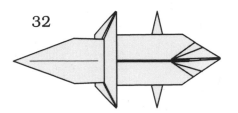

33

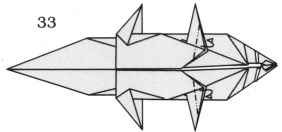

Repeat behind.

34

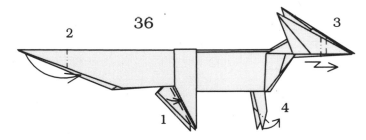

35

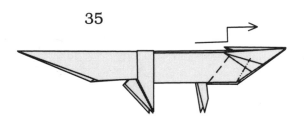

Outside reverse folds.

36

1. Tuck inside.
2. Reverse-fold.
3. Crimp-fold.
4. Reverse-fold.
Repeat behind.

37

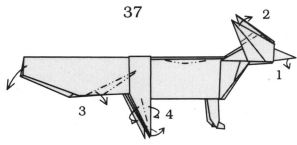

Repeat behind.

38

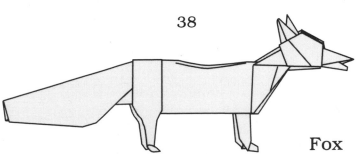

Fox

Bull

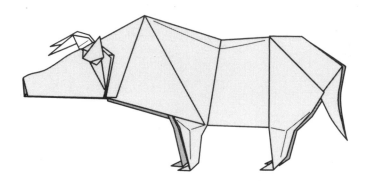

1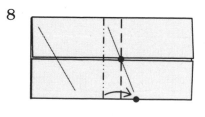

2

3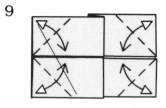

4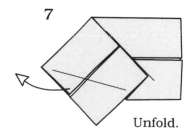

5

Fold and unfold.

6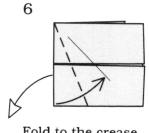

Fold to the crease while unfolding the paper from behind.

7

Unfold.

8

9

Fold and unfold.

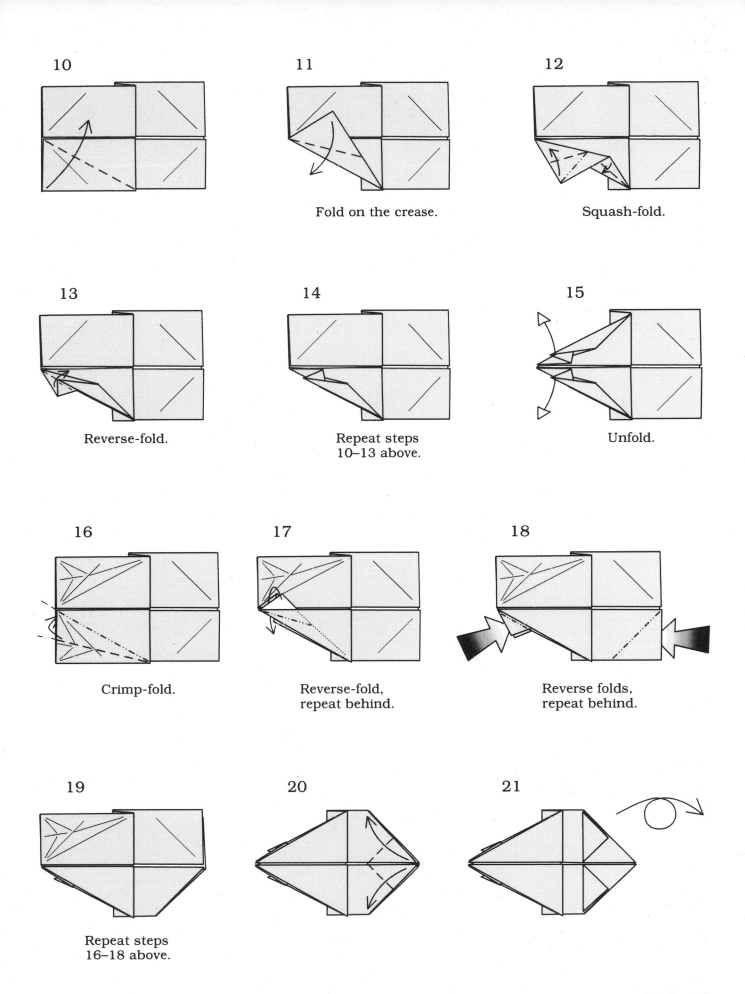

10

11

Fold on the crease.

12

Squash-fold.

13

Reverse-fold.

14

Repeat steps
10–13 above.

15

Unfold.

16

Crimp-fold.

17

Reverse-fold,
repeat behind.

18

Reverse folds,
repeat behind.

19

Repeat steps
16–18 above.

20

21

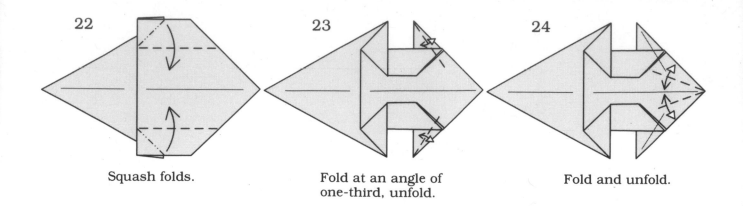

22 Squash folds.

23 Fold at an angle of one-third, unfold.

24 Fold and unfold.

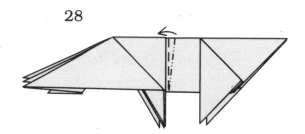

25

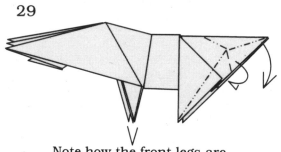

26 Crimp-fold.

27 Tuck inside, repeat behind.

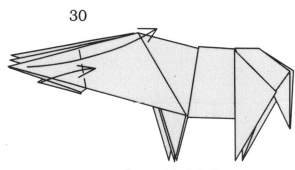

28 Open the model for this crimp fold. Crimp so that the front legs will be balanced.

29 Note how the front legs are centered. Double-rabbit-ear the tail along the creases.

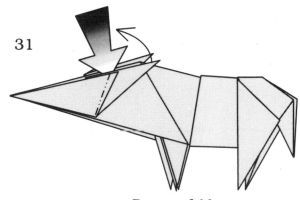

30 Repeat behind.

31 Reverse-fold, repeat behind.

32

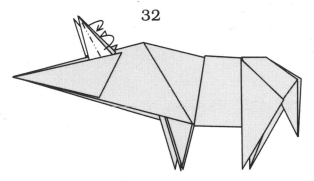

Repeat behind.

33

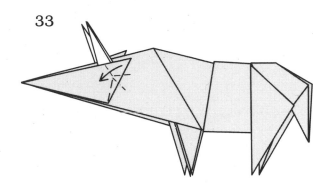

Repeat behind.

34

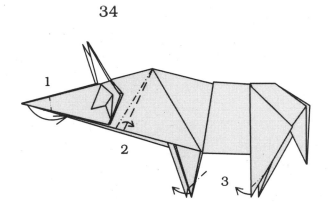

1. Reverse-fold.
2. Crimp-fold.
3. Reverse-fold, repeat behind.

35

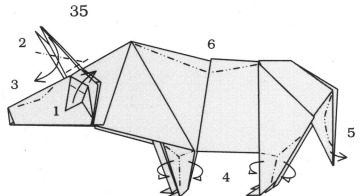

Repeat behind.

36

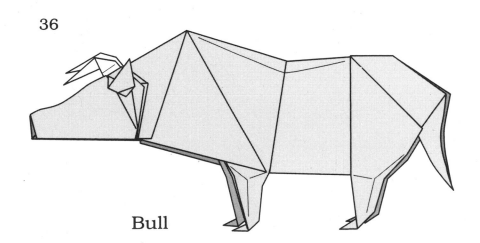

Bull

Lion

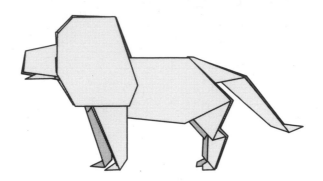

1

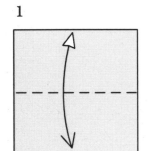

2

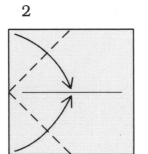

3

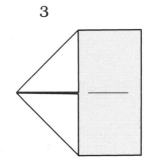

4

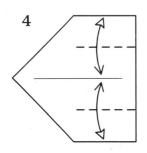

Fold and unfold.

5

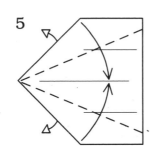

6

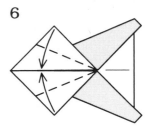

7

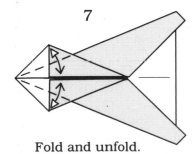

Fold and unfold.

8

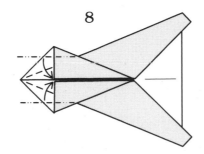

9

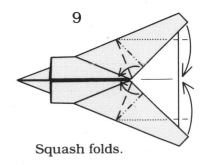

Squash folds.

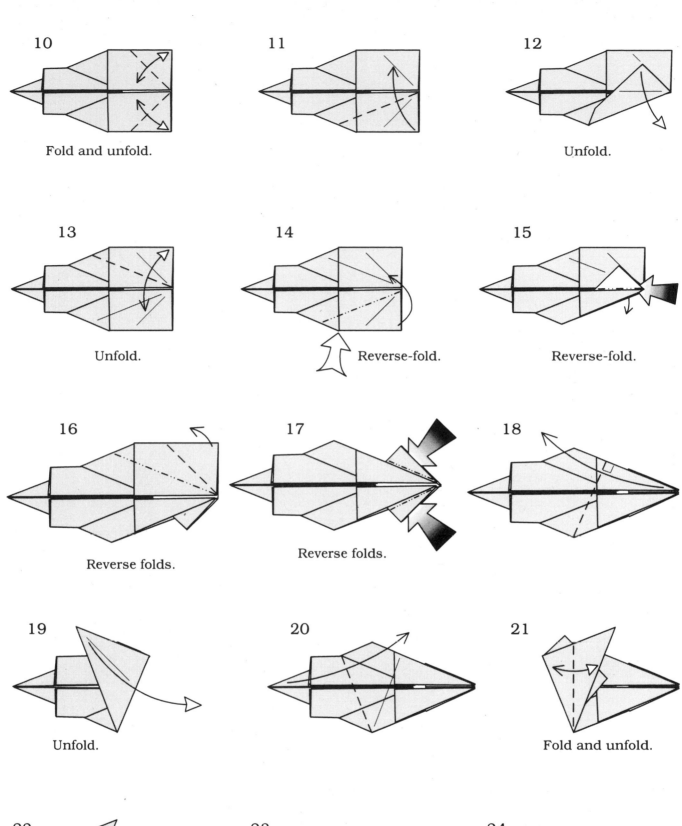

10 Fold and unfold.

11

12 Unfold.

13 Unfold.

14 Reverse-fold.

15 Reverse-fold.

16 Reverse folds.

17 Reverse folds.

18

19 Unfold.

20

21 Fold and unfold.

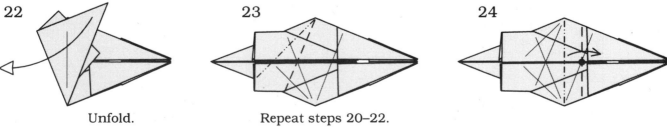

22 Unfold.

23 Repeat steps 20–22.

24

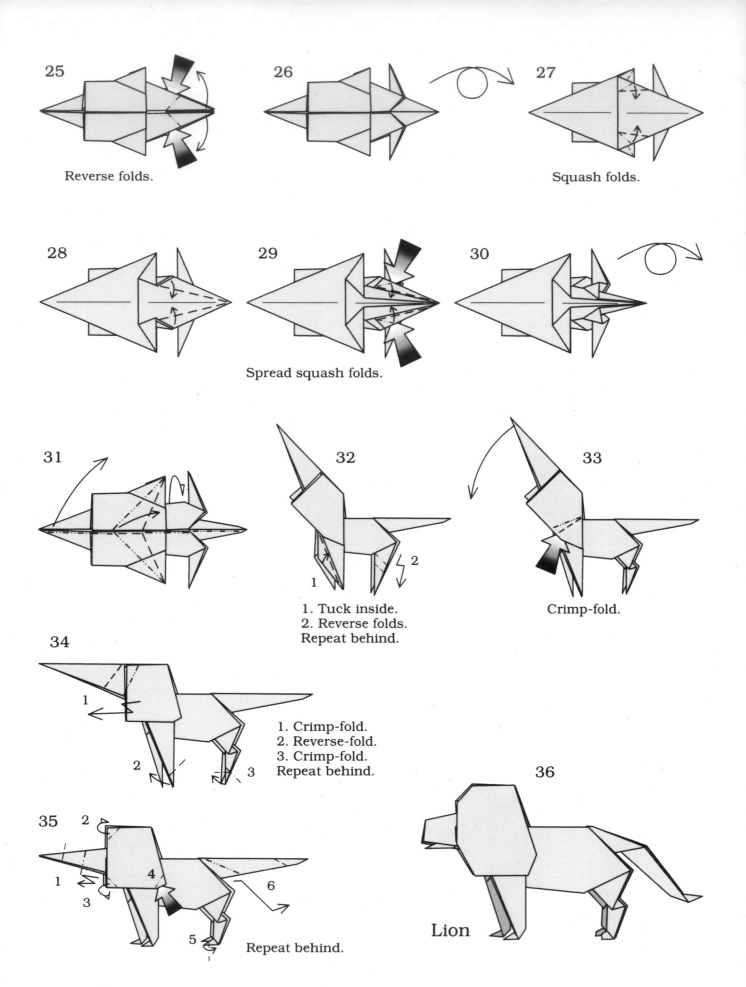

25 Reverse folds.

26

27 Squash folds.

28

29 Spread squash folds.

30

31

32
1. Tuck inside.
2. Reverse folds.
Repeat behind.

33 Crimp-fold.

34
1. Crimp-fold.
2. Reverse-fold.
3. Crimp-fold.
Repeat behind.

35 Repeat behind.

36 Lion

Elephant

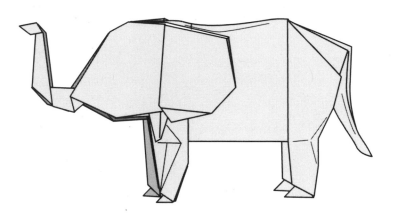

1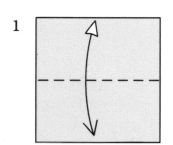

2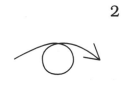

3

4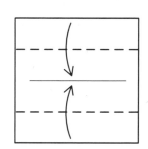

5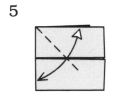

Fold and unfold.

6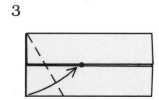

Fold to the crease
while unfolding the
paper from behind.

7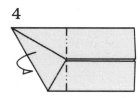

Unfold.

8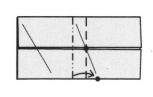

9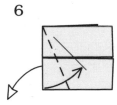

Unfold everything.

10

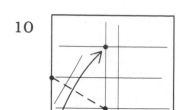

11

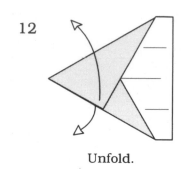

12

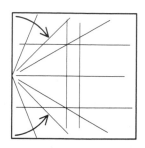

Unfold.

13

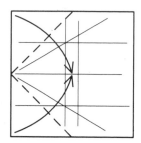

14

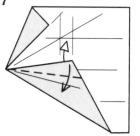

Unfold.

15

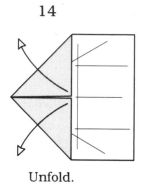

16

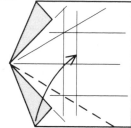

17

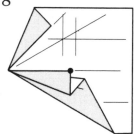

Fold down so that the
dot in the next step will
be on the center line.

18

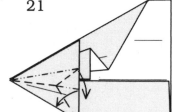

Repeat steps
16–18 above.

19

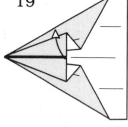

Unfold.

20

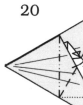

21

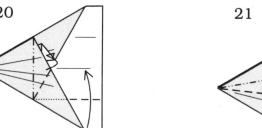

22

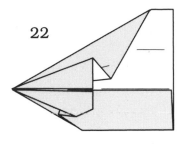

Repeat steps 19–21 above.

23

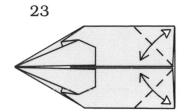

Fold and unfold.

24

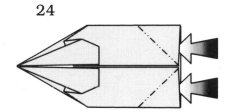

Reverse folds.

25

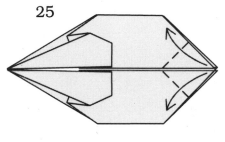

26

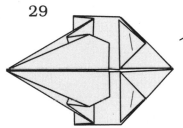

Fold to the line.

27

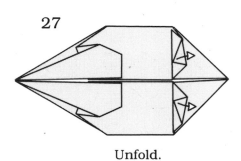

Unfold.

28

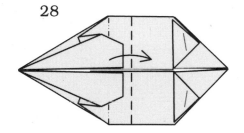

Fold on the creases.

29

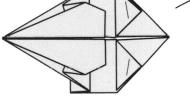

30

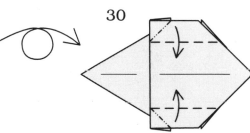

Squash folds.

31

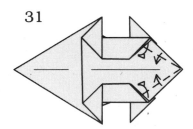

32

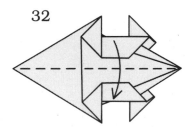

33

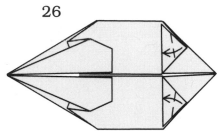

1. Tuck inside, repeat behind.
2. Double-rabbit-ear.

34

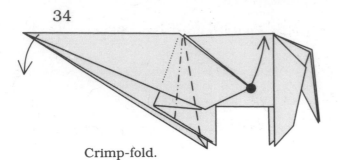

Crimp-fold.

35

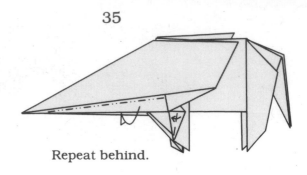

Repeat behind.

36

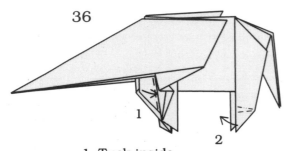

1. Tuck inside.
2. Crimp-fold.
Repeat behind.

37

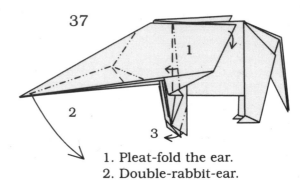

1. Pleat-fold the ear.
2. Double-rabbit-ear.
3. Reverse-fold.
Repeat behind.

38

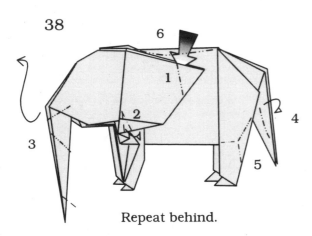

Repeat behind.

39

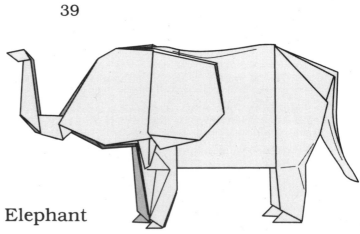

Elephant